CENTRAL PARK
A Photographic Guide

Photographs by
VICTOR LAREDO

Text by
HENRY HOPE REED

DOVER PUBLICATIONS, INC.
New York

PREFACE

This book celebrates New York City's Central Park and all that it contains within its 840 acres. For each of us there is something special to admire, enjoy or cherish. There are also probably some things to which we can object. Yet there it is. A great park, a great place, a unique monument to the vision and foresight of those who came before us and a challenge to our wisdom now.

The Central Park Community Fund

Frontispiece: The Bow Bridge and the Lake, seen from the Top of the Park Restaurant at the top of the Gulf & Western Building on Central Park West and 60th Street. The thick woods to the left and beyond the bridge is the Ramble where birds rest during their spring and fall migrations. To the northeast are former private residences on Fifth Avenue between 78th and 79th Streets. The low building with the three chimneys is the James B. Duke mansion which now belongs to the Institute of Fine Arts of New York University.

Published in Canada by General Publishing Company, Ltd., 30 Lesmill Road, Don Mills, Toronto, Ontario.
Published in the United Kingdom by Constable and Company, Ltd., 10 Orange Street, London WC2H 7EG.

Central Park: A Photographic Guide is a new work, first published by Dover Publications, Inc., in 1979.

International Standard Book Number: 0-486-23750-8
Library of Congress Catalog Card Number: 78-70152

Manufactured in the United States of America
Dover Publications, Inc.
180 Varick Street
New York, N.Y. 10014

INTRODUCTION

Central Park is one of the world's great urban parks for several reasons. It is literally in the center of a metropolitan area. It offers a splendid vantage point for viewing New York's incomparable skyline. It is easily reached by mass rail transportation (there are ten subway stations serving three subway lines along its borders, while a fourth has stations only a quarter of a mile distant). Finally and foremost, its plan ranks with the best of the wholly man-made parks.

It must be emphasized that the park is indeed a man made creation because there exists in this country the curious habit of belittling our man-made wonders when compared with those of nature. There is also the unfortunate and unwarranted tendency to compare our works unfavorably to those of other peoples, notably the Europeans. Central Park disproves both fallacies. Elsewhere, to be sure, the climate may make for greener lawns, public behavior may be more disciplined, or horticultural maintenance may be more substantial. Yet how much better, for example, is traffic controlled by the plan of Central Park than by that of the Bois de Boulogne! And how much greater is the variety of trees and shrubs, let alone the variety of terrain, than that of Hyde Park!

Among America's better man-made wonders—its highways, bridges, great public buildings, skyscrapers (a native specialty) and leafy suburbs—Central Park stands out prominently. How did it come to be, and what was the climate that produced it? Of the general attitudes which pervaded America in the second quarter of the last century, the one that had most bearing on the creation of the park was the change in the way Americans regarded nature. Where they had once rejected it, viewing it as something to be overcome, they now sought it out, even in its wild form. John James Audubon, who died in New York in 1851, spent a lifetime exploring nature, producing his famous pictures of birds. William Cullen Bryant wrote poetry extolling nature. After 1825 there gathered in the Hudson Valley painters who sought their subject matter along the river and in the Catskills and Adirondacks; the work of the Hudson River School, as it became known, hung in New York drawing rooms. The landscape architect Andrew Jackson Downing was probably the most important of all, because he engaged in the actual business of transforming nature. He laid out extensive country estates in the informal or picturesque style, and, in several very popular books, he persuaded New Yorkers (and Americans generally) that it was the only style of landscaping.

New Yorkers were swept up in a wave of excitement about nature. By the 1830s a trip up the Hudson was essential to the worshippers of the great outdoors. Travelers returning from Europe continually exclaimed about the extensive royal parks of London, Paris, Dresden and Vienna—parks which, although crown property, were open to the public. But in 1850 the city's largest park was Mount Morris (now Marcus Garvey) Park, and it covered only twenty acres. Bryant and Downing were among the first to demand that the city acquire land for a large park, the former making good use of *The Evening Post*, which he published and edited, to publicize the cause.

In the mayoralty election of 1850 both candidates came out in favor of a large park for the city, virtually insuring its creation. The winner, Ambrose C. Kingsland, took the first step the following April by asking the Common Council to initiate legislation to provide a park "which would be at once the pride and ornament of the city." As always in such matters, acquisition of land did not

Men with pick and shovel and with horsecarts tell of the simple means Olmsted and Vaux had at their disposal in transforming the park site. The view is to the south from the Mall, on which the men are working. On the left is the familiar Arsenal. To the south are, on the left, the Catholic Orphan Asylum for Boys on Fifth Avenue between 52nd and 51st Streets and, to the right, St. Luke's Hospital, also on the avenue, between 55th and 54th Streets.

follow immediately. The State legislature had authorized the power to take land for a park, but the actual site remained in question. There was even a proposal to obtain two sites, one on the East River as well as the one where Central Park stands today. Two years later permission was obtained to take the land for Central Park. In 1856 the acreage from 59th to 106th Streets was obtained. (The land from 106th to 110th Streets was acquired in 1863.) That same year it was placed in the care of the Commissioners of the Central Park.

Looking at the park today it is hard to imagine what it was like in 1856. We are familiar with the rocky outcrops, so much a feature of its landscape;

there were even more then. The ground was covered with boulders, part of the glacial till left by the receding ice sheet 15,000 years ago. Where there were no rock outcrops there were sluggish streams and pools of stagnant water. Squatter colonies were dispersed here and there, along with hog farms and bone-boiling works. It took 10,000 cartloads to remove the boulders and other loose rocks and to dump them at the park's border where they served as a foundation for the park wall.

This work was only the beginning. The next step was dealing with the cleared site. The commissioners wisely decided to hold a competition, which was announced in the fall of 1857. On April 28, 1858—the year must be considered the park's founding date—the commissioners chose the plan signed "Greensward" out of the 33 submitted. Its authors were Frederick Law Olmsted and Calvert Vaux.

Frederick Law Olmsted—his name has finally gained the familiarity it deserves—was what the Germans call a *Spätreifer* or late bloomer. He was born in 1822 into comfortable circumstances. He

had the customary education of those days and would have completed college—he went to Yale—had he not had eye trouble. Because he felt that outdoor work would be beneficial to his condition, he became a gentleman farmer, and by 1848 he was farming on Staten Island. This he supplemented by writing articles and books, the most important being observations on the slave South. A brief venture into publishing was unsuccessful. Then, in September 1857, he was named Superintendent of the Central Park with the job of continuing the preparation of the site for landscaping. At about the same time, the competition was announced. At this juncture Calvert Vaux comes on the scene.

Vaux, a professional man with a certain artistic talent, came from a background wholly different from Olmsted's. Born in London in 1824, he turned to architecture in his youth. He liked to draw, and his sketches were of sufficient quality to be exhibited. Andrew Jackson Downing, attending one such exhibition during a visit to London, was so impressed that he asked Vaux to come to this country

and become his partner. One of Vaux's first jobs on arriving was to help design the grounds of the Smithsonian Institution in Washington. Not long after, in 1852, Downing was drowned in a steamboat accident on the Hudson River. (A beautiful classical vase, designed by Vaux, stands next to the Smithsonian on the Mall to commemorate Downing.) Vaux, now on his own, continued his practice and also produced a book, *Villas and Cottages.*

Vaux had been outspoken about the need for a good plan for Central Park and had suggested the competition. When it was announced, he invited Olmsted to join him in submitting a design. It was in Vaux's house at 136 East 18th Street that the two men drew up the Greensward Plan.

Since both men had been exposed to Andrew Jackson Downing's informal or picturesque style of landscaping, it followed that this style was adopted in the Greensward Plan, and Central Park is a brilliant example of the mode. Essentially it is a way of transforming an unsympathetic terrain to imitate nature, but tamed nature, not a wild one. Olmsted and Vaux had in mind the English pastoral scene, with its mixture of meadow and clumps of trees. To this they added water in the form of ponds, streams and cascades, and they set aside certain portions for solid woods. The final result was an extraordinary variety of settings and vistas. They also gave the landscape greater diversity than found in nature by having a wide selection of specimen trees, shrubs and ground cover. Central Park, in a pattern followed in many American urban parks, contains a much greater range of plants than found in equivalent parks abroad. The designers' aim was to achieve as much variation as was possible without being visually disagreeable.

The sheer quantity of rock outcrops presented an obstacle. While Olmsted and Vaux had to rid the park of many to obtain a flat or sloping surface for turf, they also kept a good number which were skillfully incorporated into the design, contributing to the beauty of the whole park.

Of course, it is one thing to landscape a piece of land such as a private estate to serve a few, it is quite another to lay out a city park which has to welcome thousands and, on occasion, hundreds of thousands. Olmsted and Vaux had to accommodate crosstown traffic. This they did by sinking four transverse roads in such a way that they are simply not part of the park. Only when crossing or standing near them is the visitor able to see and hear the traffic which, in this day of the car and truck, is the affliction of so many parks across the country. To handle the crowds which came in carriage, on horseback and on foot, they devised a system of drives, bridle paths, and paths which kept the different kinds of traffic well separated. (The bridlepath was not in the Greensward Plan but was one of the several additions and changes made in the plan's execution.) The visitor will notice how a drive is carried over a path or a bridle path, and a footpath over a bridle path. This entailed a good number of bridges which might have intruded into the plan. Olmsted and Vaux concealed them by putting them in hollows or covering them with planting. Vaux designed each bridge differently to add variety. No two are alike.

The designers also wanted to disperse the visiting public evenly throughout the park. Thousands could visit, but they were to be scattered except at the entrances. Only the Mall, in the center of the park and extending for a quarter mile from the latitudes of 66th to 71st Streets, was reserved for crowds. This is the park's promenade. At its northern, wider end was a bandstand, replaced in 1924 by a bandshell. Meadows such as the Ballground (erroneously known as the Heckscher Playground) were set aside for play. The Sheep Meadow, called the Parade Ground in the Greensward Plan, did not attain its name until 1870, when a sheepfold (now the Tavern-on-the-Green) was built and sheep were turned out to graze nearby. Water was adopted for skating and for boating. At the southeast corner the Pond (not the Duck Pond as some improvers would have it) was reserved for swanboats such as are still found in the Boston Public Gardens. The Lake and the Harlem Meer had rowboats, and the former even had steam (and later electric) launches. The Conservatory Water at 72nd Street near Fifth Avenue was for model boats, which explains its present name, the Small Boat Pond.

In listing what might be called the active uses of the park, we must not forget the passive ones. Olmsted and Vaux regarded their design as a work of art and believed that as such it was to be enjoyed by the eye. Nothing was haphazardly sited. The bodies of water were also to be treated as mirrors (*miroirs d'eau*, the French call them) reflecting the passing clouds, being ruffled by the wind, part of nature's constant movement. Rock outcrops were to stand out in contrast to meadow or be crowned by an inviting gazebo. The many species of trees and shrubs were to be located carefully to the best advantage of form and color as well as for their growth. The weeping willow would obviously be placed near water, a tupelo or sour gum would be situated so that its silhouette could be seen fully. Along the park's West Drive was a concentration of evergreens to give color in winter. These, and other landscaping devices which escape the notice of most of us, were adopted. Many of them remain.

After the acceptance of the Greensward Plan work progressed rapidly on developing the park. (In December 1857, 1120 men had already been at work clearing the land, but by November 1858, 2600 were laboring at the task.) The first tree was planted on October 17, 1858 and people started coming into the park. In December there was skating on the lake. The Civil War slowed progress but never stopped it. In 1864 20,000 trees and shrubs were planted and visitors numbered six million. Work continued for about another decade. 1876 is generally accepted as the year when the park was finished.

The success of Central Park was overwhelming in its early years. Seeing it, other cities built their own parks and all of them were executed in the picturesque style. Olmsted and Vaux had created the Urban Park Movement which continued into the 1920s. Today Central Park is still pointed out as a brilliant example of foresight and planning, and the park's style still has influence, although much diluted.

The spotlight of history is presently on Olmsted, rather than on Vaux, because he had a phenomenal career, one which was carried on by his stepson and his son. He also chronicled it in detail, as did his heirs, by saving every piece of paper having to do with his life. Shelves of letters, plans, photographs and manuscripts are already proving a gold mine to the industrious professor and graduate student. The result is that the modest Vaux has been left in the shadow. At the start, when the two men were partners, Vaux was the prime mover, and only he has left some description of how they went about transforming a park site. His skill as a trained artist is evident in the sketches he made for the Greensward Plan, which can be seen at the Museum of the City of New York. (The plan itself is on permanent exhibition on the third floor of the Arsenal, on Fifth Avenue opposite 64th Street.) The initial sketch of the plan of Brooklyn's Prospect Park came from his hand.

Stronger evidence of Vaux's role is the fact that Olmsted's best work was executed while he was in partnership with him. Of this, far ahead of all, was Central Park, with Prospect Park as a possible rival. Prospect Park was the first result of Central Park's success; they obtained the contract to execute the design in 1866. Here again Vaux initiated their work on the project as Olmsted was in California at the time.

As partners working for the City of Brooklyn they even devised the "park-way" as an improvement on the Paris boulevard. This was not the landscaped highway of today, but a wide drive with green on either side to link the parks of Brooklyn and New York. The first one, started in 1873, was Ocean Parkway, joining Prospect Park to Coney Island.

The partnership lasted until 1872, after which the two men had irregular connections with Central

Park. This was particulrly true of Olmsted who, after 1880, spent most of his time in Brookline outside of Boston. Vaux remained in New York to serve as Landscape Architect to the Department of Parks from 1881 to 1883 and from 1888 until his death in 1895.

A third landscape architect, Samuel B. Parsons, Jr., was connected with the park. His name is familiar because he was the son of the famous Queens nurseryman after whom Parsons Boulevard was named. A graduate of Yale, Parsons worked for Vaux and was for many years Landscape Architect to the Park Department, even being Commissioner briefly. His name crops up again and again in the later history of the park.

A fourth figure—Andrew Haswell Green—must be mentioned. He was one of those men who, New Englanders by birth, gave themselves up to reform and improvement on becoming New Yorkers. Born in Worcester, Massachusetts, Green was a lawyer. He clerked for, and then became a partner of, Samuel J. Tilden, Governor of New York State and Democratic candidate for the Presidency in 1876. In 1857 Green was Treasurer of the Board of Commissioners of the Central Park and he remained on the Board until 1870. He was a leader in the fight against Boss Tweed. In the 1890s he had a key role in bringing together the Tilden Foundation, the Astor Library and the Lenox Library to form the New York Public Library. He was also given the name of "Father of Greater New York" because, more than any other, he campaigned for the amalgamation of New York and Brooklyn, and for the city's expansion, which resulted in the creation of the metropolis in 1898.

While on the park board he was a trial for Olmsted and Vaux. He was continually interfering in their work or by-passing them to push forward a favored project. And he was largely responsible for placing the Metropolitan Museum of Art in the park. Despite this side of his nature, he was one of the park's stronger defenders over the years.

Central Park was in need of defenders. From the moment the Greensward Plan was declared winner, (and no doubt before that April day) the park has been plagued by eager donors, promoters and improvers anxious to make some change which, of course, is always for the public weal. These individuals are seldom interested in taking their projects elsewhere; only in the park do they have a large captive audience and the possibility of a perpetual memorial. Battling these invasions is one of the park's traditions.

In the last century the most conspicuous invasion was that of statues. It was an obsession; donors would not be put off. A report, written in 1873 and signed by Vaux and the great painter

Frederick E. Church, stated that the park was for recreation and pleasure and not for "sepulchral memorials." The board accepted the Seventh Regiment Monument, now on the West Drive, reluctantly. An attempt was made, successful to a degree, to restrict statues to the Mall (and these to statues of literary figures).

One of the most popular features of the park, today being seriously questioned, is the Zoo. Had Olmsted and Vaux had their way it would never have been built in the park. They had wanted to demolish the Arsenal, now Park Department headquarters, which is at the Zoo's center. It is absent from the Greensward Plan. In the area around the Arsenal the park commissioners put the animals which worthy citizens insisted on giving to the city. Such was the origin of the country's first zoo.

Some projects existed a brief time and disappeared. Around 1870 concrete dinosaurs in imitations of those now found in Sydenham Park were actually made. They were about to be placed in the southwest corner of the park when, as a result of a change in administration, they were, instead, simply buried in the park. Another transient innovation, made at the turn of the century, was a miniature railroad large enough to carry children; it operated just inside the park wall from Fifth Avenue south of 110th Street. The most important addition was the great Conservatory at 105th Street and Fifth Avenue. The large glass building, with several propagating houses, fulfilled a promise held out in the Greensward Plan, which made accommodation for a conservatory at what is now popularly known as the Small Boat Pond. (Its official name is, appropriately, the Conservatory Water.) The project was followed through, although not in accordance with the plan. On the site of the present Conservatory Garden, where Olmsted and Vaux had intended an arboretum, the Department built the conservatory in 1899, no doubt having been influenced by the conservatory built in Chicago's Lincoln Park around the time of the World's Columbian Exposition of 1893. (The giant conservatory in the New York Botanical Garden in the Bronx dates from 1902.) It was a splendid structure, one that reinforced the park's emphasis on horticulture but, unfortunately, it lasted only until 1934.

The first years of this century saw the biggest change with the coming of the automobile. The drives, originally in gravel, were covered with asphalt in 1912. A late change was the introduction of special recreation facilities and equipment. Olmsted and Vaux had asked for the acquisition of a site to be reserved for active recreation, similar to the Parade Ground next to Prospect Park. They foresaw that the recreation movement, of which Central Park is recognized as the first milestone, would call for places in the park to be set aside for special sports use. Permanent tennis courts were the first. Others, such as baseball diamonds and asphalt playgrounds, followed. A bicycle path came in the 1930s. One innovation, which did not demand special equipment beyond a low fence, was a bowling green; there are now two in the northwest corner of the Sheep Meadow. The sheep which had been grazing in the meadow since 1870 were banished in 1934 and the Sheepfold was converted to the Tavern-on-the-Green. The park thus lost its most conspicuous pastoral touch. At the same time the zoo was wholly rebuilt. The biggest change of all was the disappearance of the old Receiving Reservoir of the Croton Aqueduct. This giant rectangle of water occupied the area west of the Metropolitan Museum. Having become obsolete, it was drained in 1929 and seven years later the site became the Great Lawn, now a large sports area.

While in the last century donors offered statues for the park, in this century the preferred gifts are recreational or entertainment facilities. The donor's reward is having his name attached in perpetuity to the gift, although the taxpaying public usually pays for most of the "gift." The Wollman Skating Rink (1955), the Delacorte Theatre (1962), and the Lasker Rink and Pool (1967) are three of the more conspicuous examples. One recent donor has his name in five places!

Happily there has been a distinct trend away from this self-advertising. A good example of the proper linking of the public and private sector in park improvement is the Bow Bridge on the Lake. This ancient structure, designed by Vaux in 1863 and saved by Samuel Parsons in 1911, was in danger of collapsing. In 1973 two modest donors, Lucy G. Moses and Lila A. Wallace, underwrote a restoration costing over $350,000. Similarly, the arbors near Central Park West and 72nd Street and the Pergola behind the Bandshell were repaired by the Manhattan Shops and the Five Boro Shops of the Department with lumber furnished by an anonymous donor. In the same way, due to the encouragement of such organizations as the Friends of Central Park, Central Park Task Force, Central Park Community Fund and other concerned organizations, old trees have been cared for and new specimen trees have been given by donors. One major development in tree-giving was the creation of the Pinetum (donated by Arthur Ross) in the northwest corner of the Great Lawn. In recent years the ability of evergreens to withstand pollution has occasioned much debate and some research. The pine is now being tested there to see how well its several species grow in the city climate while adding to the park's beauty.

The widespread interest and concern for Central Park have again put the focus on horticulture. Planting fashions have changed over the years. For example, older people will recall the time when hydrangeas were found in backyard and suburban gardens; now they are a relative rarity. There is one hydrangea in the park today while there were at least half a dozen at the turn of the century. When the park obtained its first trees and shrubs, evergreens formed the most conspicuous element. Many of them were quick-growing Norway spruce, put in as "nurses" to protect the slow-growing species. The policy at the beginning was to "plant thick," then to "thin quick." The latter was neglected so that, by the 1880s, the plantations were crowded and often disfigured by scraggly Norway spruce which ought to have been removed. Vaux and Parsons came up against strong opposition, notably by the press, to any thinning. But this obstacle seems to have been overcome and the park was in fine shape by 1900. The planting was considered worthy enough to be mapped and recorded in a book.

Among the trees and shrubs in the park at the turn of the century and now absent were the American hornbeam, the staghorn sumac, the Canadian redbud, the panicled dogwood, weeping silver linden, a weeping European ash, Irish yew, French tamarisk, Japanese styrac, American beech, basswood, Spanish chestnut, cedar of Lebanon and the white tree (Sorbus aria). Also present were several varieties of hydrangea where there are now only one or two bushes of one variety, a half dozen black walnuts where there is now only one, a dozen shagbark hickories where there are only two. In recent years a number of plants which had disappeared, including the Himalayan pine and the Camperdown elm, were brought back. There is now a policy of replacing a dead rarity such as burr oak or a horse chestnut with a similar variety. The Pinetum has even introduced varieties of pine such as the Japanese white pine, which has not been previously recorded in the park before. This joint effort on the part of the public and the department has been especially successful in reviving the horticultural tradition of the park. Trees, shrubs, flowers and turf, as well as water and rock outcrops, were part of the palette of Olmsted and Vaux. "Everywhere is displayed the utmost resource of the artist," wrote Ap Rhys Caparn, the landscape architect who designed the Brooklyn Botanic Garden, and he knew what he was saying. Central Park deserves the respect and care which any great work of art, but especially a great work of municipal art, deserves.

The park quickly attracted the affluent and the prosperous. By the 1880s private mansions had begun to line Fifth Avenue as far as 79th Street. On Central Park West luxury apartment buildings followed in the wake of the Dakota Apartments, which was under construction by 1880. On Fifth Avenue the mansions grew more lavish by the year. Andrew Carnegie built his at 91st Street in 1900; it is now the Cooper-Hewitt Museum. A decade later Henry Clay Frick built his at 70th Street; it now shelters the Frick Collection. In the 1920s apartment buildings took over Fifth Avenue as they had Central Park West. Today, both rank with the finest avenues in the nation. Institutions and churches, like plums in a rich pudding, are scattered along the two sides of the park. Among the outstanding are the New-York Historical Society, the Temple Emanu-El, the Church of the Heavenly Rest and the Museum of the City of New York. The beautiful park is well matched by its rich chaplet of limestone and brick.

With such opulence on its borders Central Park deserves more than the customary respect. Unfortunately, its greenswards and its *miroirs d'eau* have, in recent years, been given over to ruthless exploitation by promoters of all kinds. These promoters know that they have a captive audience and that they are assured of attention from the press, television and radio. In fact, it can be said that the media are the worst offenders because, hungry for "events," they sharpen the promoters' greed. When television camera crews are sent to other parks, when newspaper editors assign reporters to "events" outside Central Park, when the workers in publicity mills look at the rest of the city, then will this great park be spared the destructive invasions. Then, once again Central Park will be able to fulfill its purpose of providing solace, repose and quiet joy for the people of New York.

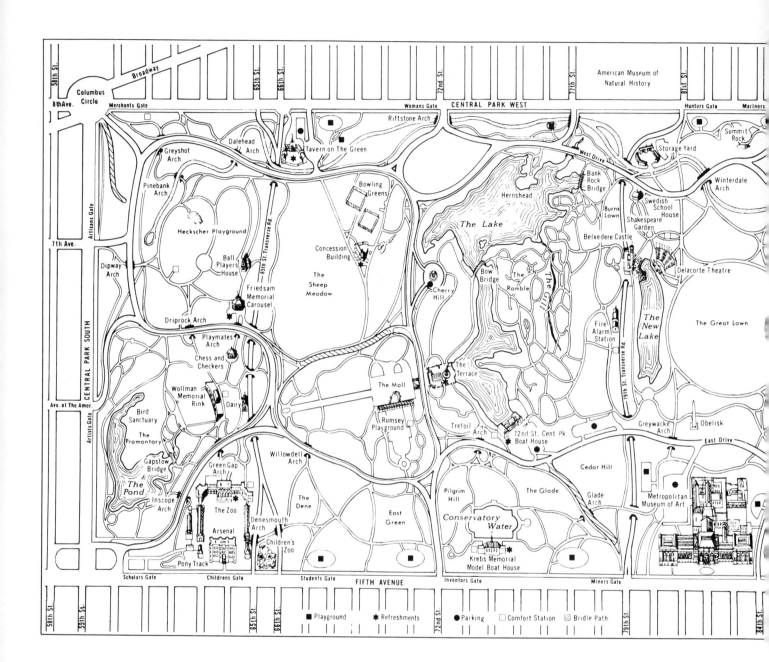

MAP OF CENTRAL PARK
by Ken Fitzgerald

A view southeast across the Sheep Meadow features the buildings of Central Park South.

1

Opposite: Looking northwest to the Gapstow Bridge. The stone bridge, designed by Howard & Caudwell and dating from 1896, replaced the original wooden one by Calvert Vaux. The Art Deco towers of the Majestic at Central Park West and 72nd Street rise in the distance. The riprap shore and the path were installed in the 1950s. **Above:** The original Gapstow Bridge at the Pond in an early view taken by an unknown photographer. *(Museum of the City of New York.)*

Above: The Dairy, built in 1870, originally provided park visitors with milk and other refreshments. Shown here in a view by an unknown photographer, it was designed by Vaux in the "Hudson River Gothic" style once considered essential in a picturesque park. When several supports were damaged by a truck in 1955, the porch was removed. A set of measured drawings for the porch and buildings is on hand for use when funds become available for restoration. *(Museum of the City of New York.)* **Right:** The Dairy stands with its back to the 65th Street Transverse Road. It is presently used for storage.

Above: A free interpretation of the area near the Arsenal (at Fifth Avenue and 64th Street) in a 1862 lithograph from *Valentine's Manual*. The ducks are on the branch of the Pond now occupied by the Wollman Skating Rink. The Green Gap Arch under the East Drive looms large in this picture; it is now hidden by trees and shrubs. **Left:** The Inscope Arch spans the path that runs between the Pond and the Zoo. Vaux, who designed all the original bridges, adopted the Tuscan arch for this one of rock-faced sandstone. In the 1960s the lamppost's sodium-vapor head replaced the basket-type head which had been designed by Henry Bacon in 1907.

5

Above: The Arsenal is the first sight to greet the visitor approaching the Zoo directly from Fifth Avenue at 64th Street. Built in 1848 for the National Guard of New York State, it is now headquarters of the Department of Parks and Recreation. The eagle and cannonballs in the pediment are original, but the drums on both sides of the door and the rifle stocks of the stoop railing are part of a 1935 rehabilitation of the structure. The 1858 Greensward Plan reveals that Olmsted and Vaux did not intend to keep the building. **Opposite:** The back of the Arsenal faces the Zoo's Seal Court. The trees along this popular promenade are honey locusts, easily identified in winter by their wavy pods.

Above: The "Menagerie" was the original name for the Central Park Zoo. Wood buildings and the simplest of iron cages like those shown in this 1895 photo by Byron occupied the zoo site west of the Arsenal until 1934, when they were replaced by the present brick structures. The nation's oldest zoo came to the park by accident. It was informally inaugurated in 1862. There was a movement to relocate it north of the 96th Street Transverse Road in the 1890s because it was considered a nuisance behind the Arsenal. *(Museum of the City of New York.)* **Opposite:** Crowds gather for feeding time at the Seal Pool. The physical layout of the Zoo has been condemned by the federal government as inadequate to the animals' needs. The lamppost at the pool's edge retains the original basket-type head. On the left in the background is an ornate aviary built in 1935.

Right, Top: The Musical Clock spans the path leading to the Children's Zoo. It is the work of Andrea Spadini, who executed it in 1965. The animals rotate and move around the clock to accompanying music on the hour and the half hour. **Right, bottom:** Geese look for a handout in the Children's Zoo, which features domesticated animals such as sheep, guinea pigs, rabbits and chickens. Many of the cages are minimal, allowing the animals to be petted by the eager children.

Above: Sheep graze on the Sheep Meadow in this view taken by an unknown photographer in 1890. In the Greensward Plan this part of the park was called the Parade Ground and later the Green. Its present name was adopted when sheep were introduced in 1870. The sheep were removed in 1934, when it was claimed they had become too inbred. *(Greensward Foundation.)*

Over: A bird's-eye view of the Sheep Meadow looking southeast is provided from an apartment on Central Park West. The Plaza Hotel at Fifth Avenue and Central Park South is at the extreme right. The photograph shows how Olmsted and Vaux handled a large meadow by giving it an irregular shape and scattering trees at its edges.

The pony cart track, to the south of the Zoo, just inside the park, is easily reached from Fifth Avenue via the 61st Street entrance. The wood wall, screening subway construction, is temporary.

Children play a game of Ring-around-a-rosy on the East Green, located between the Children's Zoo and the Conservatory Water.

Opposite: The Mall or Promenade is the main formal part of the park. 1212 feet long and 35 feet wide, it runs north to the Bandshell and the Terrace on the Lake. It remains a favored gathering place, much of its attraction coming from the rows of arching hybrid elms that line both sides, framing the vista. They were planted in 1926. Sir John Steell's statue of Robert Burns (left) was unveiled in 1880. It is one of several statues of famous men of arts and letters that line the Mall, giving it the nickname of Literary Walk. **Right:** In a print from a stereoscopic view of the 1880s, mothers, nurses and children gather at one of the two cast-iron drinking fountains that stood near the Cross Drive at the north end of the Mall. *(The New-York Historical Society.)* **Below:** On a fine Sunday in 1895 an unidentified photographer took this view looking north from the south end of the Mall. Silk hats, umbrellas and canes reflect a staid generation, when people did not even consider walking on the lawns. *(The New-York Historical Society.)*

Opposite: The Terrace links the Mall and the Lake. Calvert Vaux designed it with the assistance of Jacob Wrey Mould, who did the ornamentation. It is made of yellow sandstone from Nova Scotia with occasional panels of polished granite. **Left, top:** An example of the fine stone carving at the Terrace. The pipe rail fence next to it was built around 1910. The coachman and carriage complete a nineteenth-century scene in the park today. **Left, bottom:** Another splendid example of carving at the Terrace, this one featuring pigeons in a decorative setting of leaves and fruits of the horse chestnut tree and other plants.

Above: The upper part of the Terrace overlooks Bethesda Fountain. The brick-and-granite pavement dates from 1912. The juxtaposition of the fountain, the Lake and the view of the Ramble beyond makes this one of the most attractive and popular areas in the park. **Opposite:** An arcade runs beneath the upper part of the Terrace, which is crossed by the drive, linking it with the Mall. On the ceiling are the original Minton tiles from England. In this view, the arcade's central arch frames the view of the fountain, which portrays the Angel of the Waters. Emma Stebbins, one of Henry James's "white marmorean flock," executed the work in Rome in 1865. It depicts the Biblical story of the angel who descended to the pool at Bethesda to stir the waters, giving them healing powers. The four cherubs beneath represent Temperance, Purity, Health and Peace.

Boating has been popular in the park since 1860. Rowboats have replaced the various vessels (including one gondola) that were once used, and the New York skyline has shot up around the park, but otherwise the Lake is just as full of urban mariners as it has always been. **Opposite, top:** The view southeast from the Lake. The Terrace is to the right, hidden behind the willows. Rising in the distance is the giant slab of the General Motors Building at Fifth Avenue and 58th Street. In front of it, to the left, is the Hotel Pierre, and to the right, the Sherry Netherland. **Opposite, bottom:** A view up the northeast arm of the Lake, taken by J. S. Johnston in 1894. The photograph shows the fencing that existed in the park at the time—cast-iron posts with strands of copper-coated wire. The wooden boathouse, so in keeping with the park's rustic theme, has been replaced by a less appropriate one of brick. *(The New-York Historical Society).* **Above:** The beautiful Bow Bridge, spanning the Lake between the Ramble and Cherry Hill, was designed by Vaux in 1859. One of the great cast-iron bridges of the world, it was completely restored in 1973 by the P. A. Fiebiger Ironworks and the Taylor Foundry through the generosity of Lucy G. Moses and Lila A. Wallace.

Before work began on Central Park, the site contained 42 species of trees; in 1873 there was a total of 1447. The number has declined somewhat because of the extensive use to which the park is put, but many species remain, to the delight of botanists and tree fanciers. **Opposite, top left:** This ancient London plane, one of the largest trees in the park, stands by the bridle path directly on the northeast curve of the Reservoir. **Opposite, top right:** An elm off the Mall dates back to the early days of the park. **Opposite, bottom left:** Another of the old trees in the park is the Chinese elm, near 72nd Street and Fifth Avenue. **Opposite, bottom right:** The Austrian pine,

(Pinus nigra) is the park's chief evergreen. It is easily identified by its long hard needles, two to a bundle, and by its reddish-brown bark. For years it was thought to be the only conifer that could do well in the park, but the Pinetum at the Great Lawn is now proving that many pines can flourish here. **Above:** The Japanese cherry tree is only one of the many different flowering trees and shrubs in the park. Others are forsythia, mock orange, jetbead, star magnolia, soulange magnolia, black cherry, black locust, crabapple, Japanese pagoda tree and yellowwood.

Opposite: Another Austrian pine at the Conservatory Water on an early spring day. The view shows how several activities can take place in one location at the same time. While picknickers loll in the foreground, children sail their boats on the water, people stroll—glad to be out of their apartments after the long winter—and cyclists ride along the paths.
Above: As the Japanese cherry trees flower in early spring a soccer enthusiast recovers his ball and a family takes a walk, the child clutching its balloon. In the background are the Plaza Hotel and the General Motors Building.

Right, top: A willow grows on the banks of the Pool, near the Boys Gate at 103rd Street and Central Park West. **Right, bottom:** Changing nature at the Pond. Slurry from the construction of a subway tunnel was dumped into the park's irrigation system to find its way into the Pond. Three mallards, a herring gull and a sandpiper enjoy the temporary shoal. The Bird Sanctuary, with its lush vegetation, forms a backdrop. **Opposite:** New York has many parks, but few of them are as heavily used as Central Park. Each of its 840 acres is put to use. Some forms of recreation were provided for by Olmsted and Vaux; others they did not visualize. Horseback riding as a pastime was made possible in New York City by the creation of the Bridle Path, which runs for 4.5 miles. This view looks south from the north end of the Reservoir.

Opposite: An artist at work beneath a Japanese pagoda tree. **Left, top:** Professional dog-walkers are familiar early morning sights in the park all year long. **Left, bottom:** A game at the Ball Ground on the park's west side, between the latitudes of 63rd and 65th Streets.

Above: Rock outcrops bearing the marks of the ice sheet that covered Manhattan 15,000 years ago are common in the park. Children flock to them. What better place for climbing or playing King of the Mountain? **Opposite, top left:** Chess on the Kinderberg on the latitude of 64th Street west of the Zoo. In the old days an open shelter for children stood there. Today it is a senior citizens' refuge. In the background is the Dairy. **Opposite, top right:** Birdwatchers are a common sight on spring and fall mornings in the Ramble. Over 114 different kinds of birds, among them barn swallows, pied-billed grebes, eastern phoebes, myrtle warblers, great-crested flycatchers, Baltimore orioles, scarlet tanagers, hairy woodpeckers and long-eared owls have been seen in the park in the course of a year. About 20 species, including the cardinal, nest there. **Opposite, bottom left and right:** The Friedsam Memorial Carousel, in the middle of the park on the latitude of 65th Street, is easily reached by going west from the northwest corner of the Zoo or by following a series of paths running northeast from Columbus Circle.

Central Park embraces all styles of dining, ranging from al fresco lunching on the Zoo Terrace (right, bottom) or a picnic (opposite) to the formal surroundings of the Tavern-on-the-Green (right, top). At Central Park West and 67th Street, the building housing the restaurant was designed by Jacob Wrey Mould as a sheepfold for the animals that grazed on the Sheep Meadow. After the sheep were removed it was made into a restaurant which has remained popular. It was completely renovated in 1976, and diners may now eat there amid theatrical elegance at high prices.

Right, top, and opposite: Feeding the pigeons is a year-round activity. The European rock dove, to give the bird its proper name, is an immigrant which settled long ago in Central Park. **Right, bottom:** The squirrel is another familiar resident of the park.

A detail of mounted police patrols the Bridle Path. On weekends and holidays a volunteer force of auxiliary mounted police augments the regular patrol.

As soon as the park was opened, its drives were crowded with the carriages of wealthy New Yorkers, who now had a proper setting in which to show off their splendid equipage. Those days are long past, but carriages are for rent by the hour, and a leisurely drive through the park is a favorite pastime for visitors.

Opposite, top: In 1895 Byron took this photograph of the West Drive near the southwest corner of the Lake. The popularity of driving in the park gave an impetus to the business of the carriage maker. The world-famous William Brewster of Broome Street started his business during the same decade in which the park opened and many of his carriages can be seen today in the collection of the New-York Historical Society. Approaching us we can see (left to right) a phaeton, a stanhope gig and a brougham. Receding in to the background are two cyclists and two hansom cabs. A policeman surveys the scene from his position beneath John Ball's statue of Daniel Webster (1876), and the two ladies with parasols (both apparently in mourning) bespeak an age in which sun worship was unknown. *(Museum of the City of New York.)* **Opposite, bottom:** The New York Coaching Club on a park outing on May 7, 1910, as captured by an unidentified photographer. These show coaches were known as "park drags." Olmsted and Vaux had purposely made the drives winding to discourage racing. *(The New-York Historical Society.)* **Above:** A "big snow" in 1886 brought out the sleighs, as shown in this engraving from *Harper's Weekly*. In the center, near the Webster statue, is a mounted policeman. In the background is the Dakota apartment house, which had been erected two years earlier.

Above: The path around the Reservoir, a little more than a mile and a half long, is popular with joggers. Although not strictly part of the park, the Reservoir is one of its wonders — a huge mirror which reflects the ever-changing sky and creates sweeping views from within the park. **Opposite:** On weekends and holidays the park drives are closed to automobile traffic and bicycles take over. In 1966, Irwin J. Schwartz and Henry Hope Reed suggested the innovation; a bicycle renaissance followed, today matched by the fashion for jogging.

42

Opposite, top: Music at the Bandshell on the Mall. **Opposite, bottom:** The north end of the Mall portrayed by *Harper's Weekly* in 1869. In those days, instead of the present inap- propriate Bandshell, there was a splendid polychromed band- stand designed by Jacob Wrey Mould. **Above:** Brass on the Mall, a spring rite.

New Yorkers enjoy the park year-round. A good snow, rather than keeping them at home, has always brought them into the park in large numbers. **Above:** Although named for a donor, the Wollman Skating Rink was largely paid for by the New York City taxpayer. It stands on what was originally an arm of the Pond. **Opposite, top:** In this famous photograph of ice-skating on the Lake, taken by an unidentified photographer in 1890, the Dakota is the only high structure to be seen on Central Park West. (*The New-York Historical Society.*) **Opposite, bottom:** After a snow in 1898, Byron took this photograph of children with their sled. At that time there were plenty of pines in the park, giving it some extra color during the winter. They had disappeared by the 1920s. Only today, with the planting of the Pinetum at the north end of the Great Lawn, are they again in evidence. (*Museum of the City of New York.*)

Over the years various sections of the park have been given over exclusively to one activity. **Above:** Model sailboats glide across the Conservatory Water (also known as the Conservatory Pond and the Small Boat Pond). The official name derives from the Greensward Plan, in which it was specified that the site was to have a large elaborate garden and a conservatory. **Opposite, top:** The tennis courts on the west side of the park on the line of 95th Street were installed around 1910.

Surely there are few tennis courts in the world which have so beautiful a setting. **Opposite, bottom:** In the mid-1920s a bowling green was put in the park. A second one, made of muck dragged from the Lake, was installed in the 1930s. The ancient game has a solid following and the two greens, northwest of the Sheep Meadow on the latitude of 69th Street, are busy in season.

Through the clever use of overpasses, Olmsted and Vaux were able to keep vehicular, pedestrian and equestrian traffic separate. Vaux created all of the original arches, each one having its own distinct design. **Opposite, top:** The Greywacke Arch, beneath the East Drive to the west of the Metropolitan Museum of Art and south of Cleopatra's Needle, is built of brick and Nova Scotia sandstone. **Opposite, bottom:** The Trefoil Arch beneath the East Drive bridges the path going from Conservatory Water to the Lake and the Boathouse. It is of sandstone and has a cast-iron railing. **Above:** A rather plain bridge with pipe railings crosses a small arm of the Lake, linking the West Drive at the latitude of 77th Street with the Ramble. In earlier years a more elaborate rustic bridge of oak spanned the water.

51

Opposite, and above, left and right: Delicate tendrils and flowers, ivy leaves and Gothic-shaped supports are found on the bridges over the Bridle Path near the Reservoir. **Left:** A detail of the cast-iron Bow Bridge.

Right, top: The Huddlestone Bridge, not far from the west end of the Harlem Meer. **Right, bottom:** The Glen Span, east of the Pool on the line of 102nd Street, built of Manhattan schist that was no doubt quarried in the park, replaced an earlier bridge of wood. The stream, named Montayne's Rivulet, predates the park; only a short stretch of it was kept by the park's designers. **Opposite:** A cascade on the Loch, which runs between the Pool and the Harlem Meer.

From the outset, Olmsted and Vaux were firmly opposed to the presence of statuary in the park. The erection of memorials, they argued, detracted from the rustic quality they had worked so hard to achieve. But in 1864 the first statue had been unveiled. It depicted the allegorical figure of Commerce, and was melted for scrap in World War II. A proliferation (of sharply varying quality) followed. **Opposite, top left:** The *Indian Hunter* to the west of the south end of the Mall, is one of the oldest statues still standing in the park, having been unveiled in 1869. It is the work of John Quincy Adams Ward who worked on the Washington equestrian in Union Square along with Henry Kirke Brown and who did the sculpture in the pediment of the New York Stock Exchange. **Opposite, top right:** Youngsters cannot resist climbing on Balto. The bronze dog, finished in 1925 by Frederick G. R. Roth, stands near the Willowdell Arch to the east of the Mall on the line of 67th Street. Balto was the husky who led the team which brought serum to Nome during the diphtheria epidemic of January,

1925. **Opposite, bottom left:** The Seventh Regiment Civil War Monument (1870) by J. Q. A. Ward, stands on the West Drive on the line of 69th Street. The Central Park commissioners originally opposed its installation in the park. **Opposite, bottom right:** The statue of Hans Christian Andersen (1956) by Georg Lober stands just west of the Conservatory Water. In the clement season a storyteller entertains children here on Saturdays. The Ugly Duckling at Andersen's feet has been twice stolen and recovered. **Above:** The obelisk popularly called Cleopatra's Needle, west of the East Drive behind the Metropolitan Museum of Art, actually has nothing to do with the famous Egyptian Queen. King Thotmes III of Egypt raised the 71-foot, 488,000 pound monument in 1600 B.C. in front of the Temple of the Sun in Heliopolis. The Romans removed it to Alexandria in 12 B.C. In 1877 the Khedive of Egypt offered it to New York and railroad magnate William Henry Vanderbilt had it transported and erected in the park in 1881. The obelisk's mate stands on the Thames Embankment in London.

For better or for worse, the park has been constantly changing since it was opened—some features have disappeared while others have sprung up. Additions like the Belvedere Castle were afterthoughts by Olmsted and Vaux themselves. These were in keeping with the theme of the park. Other additions, most of them made much later, are more intrusive. The rectangular Receiving Reservoir, opened in 1842, was drained in 1929. When the Depression struck, the city allowed "Hoovervilles" of squatters' huts to be built here, as well as in other parks. The site is now the Great Lawn.

The Belvedere, designed by Vaux, was built in 1869. It stands on Vista Rock, 140.6 feet above sea level, the highest point in the park. (The second-highest, at 140.3 feet, is Summit Rock near 83rd Street and Central Park West.) Vaux placed the "castle" here as a focal point for the Mall which is to the southeast. The United States Weather Bureau had equipment in the building until 1977, when it moved to a midtown location. Behind the Belvedere are the twin towers of the San Remo. The Belvedere Lake, also known as the New Lake, is all that is left of the old Receiving Reservoir.

Above: A solo dancer rehearses at the Delacorte Theatre. Beyond the stage is the Belvedere Lake. During the summer performances are given there by the New York Shakespeare Festival and various dance companies. **Opposite, top:** The wisteria arbor on the west side of the Lake is one of three which have survived. It is typical of the landscaping of Olmsted and Vaux to have such features scattered in a park.

Opposite, bottom: The oldest structure in the park, the blockhouse was one of the forts built across Manhattan to serve as protection during the War of 1812. The Cliff on which it stands is just south of 110th Street roughly on the line of Seventh Avenue. The view from the Cliff overlooks the rooftops of Harlem.

Opposite: One of several shelters on former boat landings of the Lake. In the old days steam (later electric) launches stopped at the landings. The original shelter was destroyed long ago; this was built in 1972 by the Five Boro Shops of the Park Department, under the direction of the late William Hillman. **Above:** The most elaborate of the lakeside shelters was rebuilt in 1970 using drawings made by John Barrington Bayley, the designer of the new wing of the Frick Collection. The timber for the rebuilt shelters was taken from parkway lampposts which had been replaced by metal ones.

Above: The Ladies Pavilion on the Hernshead. The poly-chromed cast-iron structure had stood for many years on Columbus Avenue as a shelter for passengers waiting for horse-cars. It was moved to this site in the 1900s. The delicate structure was entirely rebuilt by Hermann Weimann, iron founder, of Montvale, New Jersey, assisted by the maintenance forces of the Park Department. **Opposite:** The Vanderbilt Gate at the Conservatory Garden off Fifth Avenue and 105th Street was made in Paris by Bergrotte & Bauviller after designs by George B. Post. It formerly stood in front of the Cornelius Vanderbilt II mansion on 58th Street and Fifth Avenue. One of the finest specimens of wrought iron in the city, it was given to the Park Department by Gertrude Vanderbilt Whitney, founder of the Whitney Museum of American Art.

Above: The great Conservatory occupied the site of the Conservatory Garden off Fifth Avenue at 105th Street. When built in 1899 it was the nation's largest municipal conservatory and one of the city's showplaces, especially during the annual Easter exhibition of lilies. While other municipalities such as Chicago and Milwaukee have preserved their conservatories, New York, for some strange reason, destroyed this one in 1934. *(Museum of the City of New York.)* **Opposite, top:** The Samuel Untermeyer Fountain (1947) by Walter Schott, is the principal focus of the Conservatory Garden. **Opposite, bottom:** The Wisteria Pergola in the Conservatory Garden stands opposite the Vanderbilt Gate.

When the park was developed, the adjacent areas suddenly became prime real estate. Many of New York's finest and most interesting structures are thus to be found ringing the park. **Opposite:** The Hotel Plaza is one of the city's better-known caravanserais, a symbol of the luxury New York can offer the visitor. Built in 1907 to replace an earlier Hotel Plaza, it is the work of Henry Janeway Hardenbergh, the architect of the Dakota. **Above:** Victory leads General William Tecumseh Sherman at Manhattan's Grand Army Plaza at the southeast corner of Central Park. In one of America's great equestrian statues sculptor Augustus Saint-Gaudens portrays the hero of the Union Army as the conqueror in motion. The head was modeled when Sherman was still living (his residence being on 70th Street just east of Columbus Avenue) so the work has an authenticity rare among the city's statues. The statue was put in place in 1903 on a base of polished granite designed by Charles Follen McKim. It was moved 16 feet south of its original site in 1913. In the background is the Gulf & Western Building at Columbus Circle.

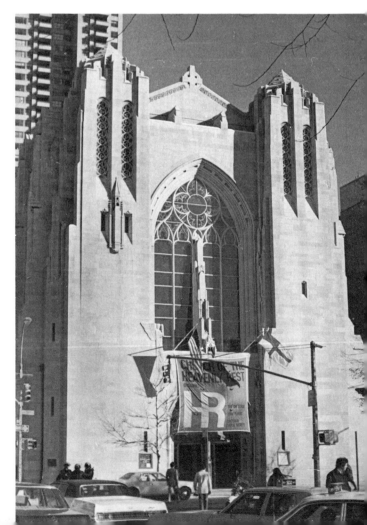

Opposite, top left: The Temple Emanu-El at 65th Street presents a sober facade to Fifth Avenue, in contrast to its interior, one of the more opulent among the city's religious buildings. Built in 1929, its architects were Robert D. Kohn, Charles Butler and Clarence S. Stein. Mayers, Murray & Philip, who were the architects of the Church of the Heavenly Rest, acted as associates. **Opposite, top right:** Shearith Israel, at 70th Street and Central Park West, is the city's oldest Jewish congregation. In 1655 the small band of Portuguese and Spanish Jews who formed the congregation landed in the city and founded the first Jewish community in lower Manhattan. The present building was built in 1897 on the designs of Brunner & Tryon, (Arnold Brunner was also architect of the oldest building of Mount Sinai Hospital on the other side of the park.) In the interior, behind these Corinthian columns, is the great hall and a reconstructed version of the first synagogue, which contains a number of old sacramental vessels. **Opposite, bottom left:** Carrere & Hastings, the architects of the New York Public Library, designed the First Church of Christ Scientist in 1903. The massive (though relatively small) structure stands on the northwest corner of 96th Street and Central Park West. **Opposite, bottom right:** Mayers, Murray & Philip, who participated in designing the Temple Emanu-El, were the ar-

chitects of the Church of the Heavenly Rest at 90th Street and Fifth Avenue. Built in 1928, it is constructed in solid masonry without any steel framing. The interior, like the exterior, is of monochrome Indiana limestone with little ornament. A tapestry of color enriches the interior when the sun shines through the brilliant blues and reds of the stained-glass windows. **Above:** The Frick Collection is one of the nation's great art museums. It has two virtues: it is small; its paintings are mixed with sculpture, furniture, procelain and other objects much as the founder, Henry Clay Frick, desired. Art-historical pigeonholing and the clinical approach are absent. Designed by Carrere & Hastings, it was built in 1913–14 at 70th Street and Fifth Avenue as a residence for Frick, who had made his millions in coal, coke and steel in Pittsburgh. After his death and the death of his widow the residence was skillfully transformed into a museum by John Russell Pope, architect of the Theodore Roosevelt Memorial at the American Museum of Natural History. The sculpture is the work of the Piccirilli brothers, one of whom, Attilio, did the sculpture for the Maine Monument at the southwest corner of the park. In 1977 a wing designed by John Barrington Bayley, with G. Frederick Poehler and Harry Van Dyke associates was added.

Right, top: New York is fortunate in having two institutions devoted to its history: the New-York Historical Society and the Museum of the City of New York, shown here, which stands between 103rd and 104th Streets. Of particular interest is its collection of city views, including one of the most extensive collections of photographs of the city as well as a large collection devoted to the theater. John D. Rockefeller, Jr. and the railroad financier James Speyer were among its principal founders. The building, designed by Joseph H. Freedlander, dates from 1932. **Right, bottom:** The New-York Historical Society is an institution of national importance. Here are preserved large collections of the papers of George Washington, of the architectural firm of McKim, Mead & White, of De Witt Clinton and many others. York & Sawyer were the architects of the building, which was constructed in 1908. It stands on Central Park West between 76th and 77th Streets. **Opposite:** The Theodore Roosevelt Memorial by John Russell Pope forms part of the American Museum of Natural History at Central Park West between 77th and 81st Streets. The architect adopted the Ionic order for his columns which are given a monumental stance by being set on high bases. The equestrian statue of our 32nd President is by the sculptor James Earle Frasier. The museum, the country's finest devoted to natural history, has few rivals in the world.

Opposite, top: The Solomon R. Guggenheim Museum, built in 1957–59 between 88th and 89th Streets on Fifth Avenue, is New York's sole public building by Frank Lloyd Wright. The genius of the Western prairie is said to have designed this massive concrete structure for another site, a fact which explains the absence of windows overlooking the park. **Opposite, bottom left:** Andrew Carnegie, who wooed his bride while riding horseback in Central Park, built this large mansion at the turn of the century. With the house on 91st Street and Fifth Avenue and the garden on 90th, it was a throwback to an earlier generation when many houses on the avenue were set in open lots. In this mansion the great philanthropist gave away his millions to libraries, churches and other institutions. It now houses the Cooper-Hewitt Museum, the Smithsonian Institution's National Museum of Design, one of the great decorative arts museums of the world. **Opposite, bottom right:** Fifth Avenue, at one time in its history, could boast an encyclopedia of styles in its mansions. The Jewish Museum is housed in this Gothic survivor, built in 1908 for the great banker and philanthropist, Felix M. Warburg. The architect was C. P. H. Gilbert. **Above:** The Metropolitan Museum of Art, one of the world's largest art museums, now occupies 10 acres of the park. Its Fifth Avenue facade ranks with the best of the American Renaissance. The imperial note was set by the architects Richard Morris Hunt and Joseph Howland Hunt in 1894 by using Corinthian columns on a high base with a high embellished attic. (The expansive flight of steps is a recent addition.) The wing to the south is a later addition by McKim, Mead & White. The Empire State Building is visible in the distance.

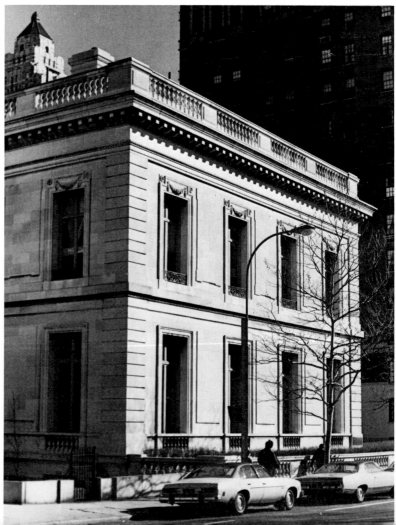

Right, top: The International Center of Photography, at No. 1130 Fifth Avenue, now occupies this brick-and-marble building, designed by Delano & Aldrich in 1914 as a residence for Willard Straight, the banker-diplomat who founded *The New Republic*. The comparatively simple Georgian-style house represented a trend away from the "Fifth Avenue Palatial." **Right, bottom:** James Buchanan Duke, the tobacco and electric-power magnate whose endowment enlarged Trinity College in Durham, North Carolina, into Duke University, did not stint when it came to architecture. For his New York mansion on 71st Street and Fifth Avenue he turned in 1910 to Horace Trumbauer of Philadelphia, one of the great architects of the American Renaissance. The beautiful residence is in the French Classical style which Trumbauer favored for most of his residences. Doris Duke, the millionaire's only child, gave the mansion to the Institute of Fine Arts of New York University.

Above, left: The Century Apartments, 25 Central Park West, are typical of the luxury buildings that flank the park. Built in 1931, the Century was designed in the Art Deco style. **Above, right:** One of the oldest surviving apartment houses in the city, the Dakota remains among the finest. It was designed in 1879 by Henry Janeway Hardenbergh, the architect of the Hotel Plaza, for Edward Clark, counsel for the Singer Sewing Machine Company. When it was built on the northwest corner of Central Park and West 72nd Street, the neighborhood was virtually bare of dwellings except for a few wooden houses and squatters' shacks. Its name is supposed to have come from the fact that, when it opened, it was so far out of the built-up portion of the city that it might as well have been in the Dakota Territory.

Right, top: The Maine Monument stands at Columbus Circle at the southwest entrance to the Park. Through the efforts of the newspaper magnate William Randolph Hearst this monument was raised in 1913 to commemorate the U.S.S. *Maine* which was sunk in Havana Harbor on February 15, 1898, precipitating the Spanish-American War. The beautiful sculpture is the work of Attilio Piccirilli, one of the Piccirilli brothers who did the sculpture of the Frick Collection building. H. Van Buren Magonigle was the architect. The bronze figures and chariot on the top are purportedly cast of bronze from Spanish guns. On one side of the monument is a small tablet cast from a scrap of metal taken from the *Maine*. **Right, bottom:** This rare rostral column, with its statue of Columbus by Gaetano Russo, was raised at Columbus Circle as part of a belated celebration of the four-hundredth anniversary of the explorer's discovery of America. Another rostral column (so-called because it is adorned by *rostra*, or ships' prows) is on the campus of the United State Naval Academy in Annapolis, Maryland. The blank-walled building in the background, opened in 1965 as the Gallery of Modern Art, is now the headquarters of the city's Department of Cultural Affairs. Edward Durrell Stone, one of the architects of the Museum of Modern Art, designed the building. **Opposite:** Central Park South looking east to Fifth Avenue. On the right is the north facade of the Hotel Plaza. The thin white sliver is a corner of Edward Durrell Stone's General Motors Building. The structure which takes command in this view along the south edge of the park is the Sherry-Netherland Hotel, a tower inspired by the pictures of Maxfield Parish. Built in 1927, it is the work of Shultze and Weaver who designed the Waldorf Astoria, as well as many other hotels.

BIBLIOGRAPHY

Clarence C. Cook, *A Description of the New York Central Park* (Reprint of 1869 edition by Arno Press, New York) 1972

The Central Park Book, written by Elizabeth Barlow with Vernon Gray, Roger Pasquier and Lewis Sharp (Central Park Task Force, New York) 1977

M.M. Graff, *Tree Trails in Central Park* (Greensward Foundation, New York) 1970

Thomas Hanley and M.M. Graff, *Rock Trails in Central Park* (Greensward Foundation, New York) 1976

Frederick Law Olmsted, Jr. and Theodora Kimball, *Frederick Law Olmsted, Landscape Architect,* *1822-1903.* See Volume 2: *Central Park As a Work of Art and As a Great Municipal Enterprise, 1853-1895* (Reprint of 1928 edition by Arno Press, New York) 1970

Frederick Law Olmsted's New York, text by Elizabeth Barlow, illustrative portfolio by William Alex (Whitney Museum of American Art/ Praeger Publishers, New York) 1972

Louis Harman Peet, *Trees and Shrubs of Central Park* (Manhattan Press, New York) 1903

Henry Hope Reed and Sophia Duckworth, *Central Park: A History and a Guide* (Second edition, Clarkson N. Potter, Inc., New York) 1972